Thoughts for a Rainy Day

# Thoughts for a Rainy Day

Poems by

Fred Skolnik

Cover design by Shay Culligan

ISBN: 978-1-954353-93-0

Kelsay Books
502 South 1040 East, A-119
American Fork, Utah, 84003

# Acknowledgments

*Boston Literary Magazine (2015):* "Evolution"

*Eskimo Pie (2012):* "Fleeting Thoughts," "Ideas and Poems," "The Lilac," "Thought for the Day"

*Free Verse (2009):* "My First Rimbaud"

*Hacksaw (2009):* "Draft for a Haiku"

*Oak Bend Review (2009):* "The Second Hand"

*Piker Press (2015):* "It Will Come," "Those Who Die Best," "A Writer's Legacy"

*Poetry Quarterly (2015):* "Perspective"

*The Satirist (2015, 2016) (writing as Fred Russell):* "Bleistein at the Royal Ballet," "Pro Ball"

*Word Riot (2012):* "The Kiss"

# Contents

# Dirge

At the end of my days
I withdrew into myself
To contemplate the questions
I had not answered
In a universe
Devoid of meaning
Just as my life might have been
Without meaning
Had I not redeemed it
And still my fortuitous presence
In this universe
Stopped me cold
For I was alone
While not alone
Insecure in the larger cosmic sense
While seemingly secure in home and country
For the planets hurtle through space
In their blind orbits
Following the fleeing stars
And there is nothing to forestall a holocaust
And then there would be
Nothing ever again
And no one to regret it.
We are alone
Specks of flesh and bone
In an eternal night
In a cold, cold place
And there is nothing beyond this
And there was nothing
Before this
And I am there
Deceived
By the rays of the sun

And the rustling of a leaf
To believe
That one thing is connected
To another
In a conscious
Design
Whereas everything is given
Inexplicably
And there is nothing
To guarantee its permanence.
How cold it is
To be alone
When you are not alone
To contemplate a universe
In which
There is neither a before
Nor an after
To be imprisoned
Inside yourself
Waiting for your end
Condemned to extinction
As though on a whim
For just as I was blessed
With mortal life
For no real reason
So might I have lived forever
Or not at all.
I contemplate
Things as they are
But cannot penetrate them
Things that are at once
Opaque and transparent

But do not yield
Their secrets.
I mean
The world itself
Spinning like a top
Without reference
To its inhabitants
I mean
The depthless universe
Rolling on and on
Like the green fields
Of summer
In a dream.
It is there
But it is not there
It cannot be grasped
But only imagined
And I am here
Surrounded by
Familiar objects
Detached from the world
For I could be anywhere
In a capsule in deepest space
And feel safe inside
Within its four walls
As I follow the stars
Untouched by their destinies
Living in the sealed room
As well as inside myself
Where ephemeral thoughts
Surge or drift through my head
Being only voices

Or pictures on a screen
So small
That they cannot be measured
Being tiny points
In the folds
Of the brain
That contain the universe.
Once I was young
And now I am old
But that is not the point
For one is either
Here
Or not here
Whether weak or strong
And the mind will race
Or sputter
Until the dying
Of the light.
I hear
A roar
Or a rumble
Outside
It could be thunder
Or a plane in the sky
Just passing by
Then it is gone
And I am alone again
But there is music too
It is inside me
And outside as well
We invented it
So it will die with us

As will our thoughts
When the last book is burned
Beneath a blazing sun
And the machines are wrecked
And the sky falls in.
Such is the end
Of all that is
And will ever be.
I cannot connect
This peaceful day
With the primal chaos
That reaches
The end of time.
It must be the former
That is the anomaly
And therefore transient
While the night
Is immeasurably long
Though it too
Must end.
Now I return
To my beginnings
Like a child in the womb
Comprehending nothing at all
And counting for less
In the eternal scheme.
Why is the darkness there
Outweighing the light
And no less real
Though neither exists
Outside the boundaries
Of my mind?

Only, in myself
Do I exist
Though I see things
As though outside myself.
There is nothing
Beyond this
Which makes me
Lonelier still
Despite the voices
From without
For I do not know
Why I am here.
Just live, you say
Well, yes
That is what
I gladly do
But certainly
One must think
And wonder too
I look toward
The heavens
And see nothing there
For air is without color
And is everywhere
Whether dark or light
Whether day or night
And the wind blows too
Whether weak or strong
And the sky is usually blue
Though that is an illusion
As we may fly
Beyond it

Into that endless sphere
Which is no less a figment
Of the imagination.
For we are alone
In this cold and empty place
Where sparks of light
Flicker
In the darkness of the night
And then expire
Leaving an idea of themselves
Implanted in the mind.
I sit in my garden
Watching the leaves
In the trees.
There is no before
Or after
There is only
The moment
That I inhabit
For all time
Is the present time
Eternally expanding.
How then do I die
If once I lived?
I die
In the same moment
That I lived.
For now I was there
And now I am not
Like a fly
That is swatted
Creeping on a wall.

The paradox of life
Is that
At one and the same time
It is
Everything
And for nothing.
The two states
Of being
And nonbeing
Are absolute
And therefore unbridgeable
Though one leads into the other.
Now you are there
Now you are not
You appear
And then you disappear
Without crossing a line
As though dissolving
In air.
What I see
I see
Only now
For all moments
Are the present moment.
The world is not
A slide show
But a continuum
Unbounded
By the hours
Of the clock.
I exist
Always
In the present moment

So that
Whatever appears before me
Appears now.
Now I see
An image
In my head
It is not
A picture on the wall
Or a face
In the crowd
But hangs clearly
Though insubstantially
In the infinite space
Of my mind.
I will not decipher
The secrets of the universe
I will not
Plumb its depths
Or grasp
Its immensity
Which is beyond
My reach
I will stare
At the sky
And imagine
That it is
In my head
And that will be
The place
Where I reside
And there I will
Create

A universe
Of my own
No less vast
Than the one
I cannot know.

# My First Rimbaud

Everyone knows New Directions
I mean the publishing house
They brought out
Rimbaud and Baudelaire
Lorca, Ferlinghetti, others
When we were young
Quality stuff
In glossy black
A stark look
And the volumes slim
As poetry should be
Giving extra weight to the words
Making you linger over them
To get your money's worth

I remember the feeling
Of first looking into Rimbaud
*Jadis, si je me souviens bien*
The myth was even better than the poem
I could recite the chronology
Like a nursery rhyme
Izambard and Verlaine
Java, Aden and Harar
Cancer and delirium
And the early death
It has stayed with me all these years
That feeling of opening a door
And finding a world within

# The Second Hand

It happens sometimes
That I look up at the clock
Just when the second hand
Pauses between one tick
And another
So that everything seems to stand still
In that moment
And I have enough time
To wonder
If the clock has not stopped.
It is amazing how much
Can go through your mind
From one second to the next.

And while clearly
A life cannot be lived
In such a pause,
Requiring time
To stretch itself out,
Memory can,
Requiring no more
Than a spark of light
To give a sign
That contains the whole.

# Draft for a Haiku

A shoot (grew out of) on a
(The) hoary branch
(Of a giant tree).
I (stood and) watched it (for a while)
And (then I) went away.
(Fifty years have passed.)
Is it still there?

# The Kiss

When Binny's best friend
Came into the room
I desired her again.
We sat on the bed
Chatting innocently
And then I thought
To kiss her
But she turned her head away
At the critical moment.

And if I had kissed her then
So much would have been different.
She would have told Binny
I am sure of that
And Binny would have
Called the wedding off
And these children that we have
Would not have been born
And I would not have seen
The places I've seen
And I would not have lived
The life I've lived.

# Fleeting Thoughts

I sit poised
Like a lion set to pounce
Or hunt actively
Like a lion on the prowl
Instinct guides me
But the thoughts race by
Like gazelles and wildebeests
And I must seize them
Before they elude me

## Ideas and Poems

Ideas die
They fade like the light of day
Are dissipated like vapor
Disperse like smoke or fog
Dissolve like the fragrance of a flower
They lose their force
Relax their rigorous hold on the imagination
Slip from memory
Vanish into thin air
If you do not give them permanent shape

A poem is such a permanent thing
It fixes ideas forever
Pins them down
Gives them immortality

# The Lilac

A lilac on my lilac bush
Did not expire in early May
But persevered
For weeks and weeks
Beyond its given time.
It did not fade or wither
But stood up proud and strong
As if to say,
"I have defied the universe,
Achieving immortality."

I celebrate this triumph.
I look out my window every day
To see if it still stands.
For such is the dream
Of all of us:
To be overlooked by fate,
To stand forever,
Inexplicably.

# Thought for the Day

No one seems to realize
That we stand in the same relation
To the new century
As people living a hundred years ago
Stood to theirs.
Once we pitied them
For living in such an ancient time
As though in the bottom of a well
Seeing only a patch of sky
That was the future.
And now here we are ourselves
Inhabiting the same point in time
Standing before an unknown historical future
Whose inevitable horrors
Cannot even be imagined.

# Evolution

First came the rock
And then came the tree
And then came we
Some sludge in a pond
Dressed up in skin
And later some bone
And a mouth
That opened and closed
And could even whistle
And hands that made things
Like smartphones and diet coke
You needed a brain for that too
And thank God we had one.

# Bleistein at The Royal Ballet

As boorish as it sounds
I have to say
That there *is*
An element of silliness
In the classical male ballet.
I mean
What exactly
Is the point
Of jumping high into the air
And banging your ankles together
Like a demented au pair?
And forget the full basket
And chiseled derriere
Of men in their underwear.

# Pro Ball

Here's how it works:
It starts in the pickup games
In the schoolyard or the park
Where everyone can see
That you're a player
And before you know it
You're on some kids' team
In an organized league
And you're a genuine star
And then you're in high school
And the scouts start coming around
And you get signed
To a big league contract
After a year or two
In the minors
And when people look into the dugout
They see you there
Among grown men
In children's pajamas
Spitting on the ground
For three straight hours
And occasionally
Patting each other's asses.

# Perspective

Born in 1940
I could never imagine
As a child
Seeing
The new millennium
And certainly not
The year
2015.

Born at such a distance
From the beginning of centuries
I also looked back at 1915
As a time immeasurably remote
Thinking
What a terrible place
That must have been
To be.

And here I am now
In that same place
Relatively speaking
Feeling
In an odd way
That I belong to a time
That will soon be
Ancient history.

# It Will Come

All good things
Come to an end,
Aunt Rose used to say,
Little knowing
That she had uncovered
The ultimate truth of things,
Something beyond Newton
And even Einstein,
Though we cannot fully grasp it.
I mean, Time runs out
And the universe too will end
And then there will be nothing
Ever again.
It seems irrelevant now
Just as our own deaths do
When we are young
But then the day is upon us
And all our years are behind us
And the unthinkable is there before us
Waiting at the door.

# Those Who Die Best

Given the time to get ready,
compulsive people die easily.
They find the idea
of putting their house in order,
tying up loose ends,
finishing up unfinished business
very appealing.
For them,
dying is the ideal way
to end a life.

# A Writer's Legacy

These books
That I leave behind
Are like ashes
In an urn
Giving me
An eternal presence
But also a voice
To speak
To those I loved
In intimate communion
Long after I am gone

I am there
Everything I thought and felt
Everything I was
Preserved forever
Made tangible and resonant
Living
In the hearts and minds
Of those I touched
When I was here
And giving me
A kind of immortality

# About the Author

Fred Skolnik is the author of 6 novels: *The Other Shore, Death,* and *Basic Forms* under his own name, and *Rafi's World, The Links in the Chain,* and *The Nightmare* under his Fred Russell pen name. His stories, essays, and poems have appeared in around 200 journals. A collection of his longer stories called *Americans & Other Stories* appeared in 2017 and a 1,000-page novel of his covering Jewish life in the 20th century via Poland, the Holocaust, and the State of Israel will be published in Spring 2022 by Addison and Highsmith. He is also the editor in chief of the 22-volume second edition of the *Encyclopaedia Judaica,* winner of the 2007 Dartmouth Medal.

www.ingramcontent.com/pod-product-compliance
Lightning Source LLC
Chambersburg PA
CBHW071752090426
42738CB00011B/2667